JANET YELLEN:

Challenge Accepted

The views and opinions expressed in this book are solely those of the authors and do not reflect the views or opinions of Gatekeeper Press. Gatekeeper Press is not to be held responsible for and expressly disclaims responsibility of the content herein.

This manuscript represents the opinions of the authors and not that of the Federal Reserve.

Janet Yellen: Challenge Accepted

Published by Gatekeeper Press
2167 Stringtown Rd, Suite 109
Columbus, OH 43123-2989
www.GatekeeperPress.com

We are grateful to Janet Yellen for her unwavering support of this project.

Library of Congress Control Number: 2022936330

ISBN (hardcover): 9781662915079
ISBN (paperback): 9781662915086
eISBN: 9781662915093

JANET YELLEN:
Challenge Accepted

Emily Engel & Lauren Fredericks

gatekeeper press
Columbus, Ohio

Dear Reader,

Every day I use my knowledge of economics to shape public policy in a way that helps people. Whether teaching future economists at leading institutions, serving in presidential administrations, or leading the Federal Reserve and the United States Treasury, I strive to use economics to to make the world a better and safer place. Balancing professional obligations with personal responsibilities, while breaking down barriers to become the first female Chair of the Federal Reserve System and the first female Treasury Secretary, has not been easy. But the rewards of hard work far outweigh the costs, and if I can do it then so can you! May you always have the courage to follow your dreams, persevere in the face of challenges and adversity, and recognize the importance of being kind and helping other people.

Best,

Janet L. Yellen

Bay Ridge, Brooklyn, a working-class neighborhood in New York, was a melting pot of different cultures in the early 1950s where young Janet Yellen grew up mixing her Jewish identity with the cultures of her neighbors. She would gaze out of her bedroom window on the second floor of her family's cozy brownstone watching people, mostly men, hurrying up and down the street to their jobs at nearby factories and warehouses. Janet thought about the process of working, earning, and spending money.

Janet's father, a doctor, often treated patients even if they could not pay him. She would listen to her parents discuss patients who had lost a job and did not have enough money to buy food. This bothered Janet a lot. It did not seem fair!

Janet was proud that her parents allowed patients to pay what they could. But, she wondered: what could she do to help people earn a steady income so that they could buy food to eat, pay their bills, and save for emergencies? Janet could not imagine at that time how her quest to answer this question would whisk her away on many exciting adventures for the rest of her life!

As Janet grew older, one question bothered her: Why do some people have jobs and make a lot of money while others struggle to pay their bills? These thoughts formed the beginning of her interest in economics, the study of how people make decisions to use money and resources.

Janet studied hard and graduated at the top of her high school class. She attended Brown University, an Ivy League School, with a beautiful campus full of Gothic architecture, arched windows and iron spires. One day, while listening to a lesson about savings, wealth, and poverty, Janet thought about her father's patients who had worried about losing their jobs. Janet's passion to help people find and keep a job led her to Yale University for graduate school where she continued to study economics. Janet enjoyed the long hours in the library learning about what caused people to lose jobs and what she could do to help. At graduation, looking across the sea of black graduation robes, Janet, the only woman in her graduating class, felt excited that she now had the skills she needed to help people.

To help prepare the next generation, Janet took a job teaching economics. She enjoyed working as a professor, but when Janet was offered the opportunity to serve on the Federal Reserve Board of Governors and then as Chair of the Council of Economic Advisors, she accepted.

One day a letter came from the Federal Reserve Bank of San Francisco offering her the chance to become its President. Janet would be the first woman to hold this job! And, she realized that as a Reserve Bank President she could continue helping people by making policies that led to the creation of jobs. After all, part of the Federal Reserve's mission is to make sure that anyone who wants a job can find one.

Walking down Market Street lined with majestic skyscrapers on her first day of work as the Federal Reserve Bank of San Francisco's President, Janet had butterflies in her stomach. Did she know enough to be the President of the Federal Reserve Bank of San Francisco? Inspired by the passion to help people, however, Janet soon let the butterflies fly away so that she could concentrate on finding solutions to keep people working.

As head of the Federal Reserve Bank of San Francisco, Janet paid close attention to the needs of the people who worked there. Sitting in comfy chairs with a fresh cup of coffee in hand, Janet hosted "Java with Janet" to listen to their thoughts and concerns, adopting her father's practice of listening to people's stories. Janet knew that it would be hard to help people if she didn't understand their problems.

This experience added to Janet's understanding of and appreciation for jobs and the economy. A big part of her role as Bank President was gathering policymakers in the marble-columned hallways of the Federal Reserve building to discuss the economy. Janet knew that their decisions would directly affect people living and working in the United States and across the globe.

Janet's leadership at the Federal Reserve Bank of San Francisco caught the attention of United States President, Barack Obama, who appointed her as the first female Chair of the Federal Reserve Board of Governors. She chose to be called "Chair" instead of "Chairman", making the title gender neutral. As she stood to take the oath of office, with her right hand in the air, Janet felt exhilarated – she knew she could help even more people than ever before.

As Chair, Janet worked hard to make sure people who wanted to work could find a job and earn a paycheck. She listened intently to her colleagues in order to help make the best policies for the country's economy. When she left the Federal Reserve in 2018, Janet was proud that the United States had the lowest number of people looking for a job in nearly half a century!

Since leaving the Federal Reserve, Janet has continued her mission to help others and is a quiet pioneer of women in the workplace. She is now starting a new chapter as Treasury Secretary. Stay tuned to see what she accomplishes next!

FORMER FEDERAL RESERVE CHAIRS:
Janet Yellen, Alan Greenspan, Ben Bernanke, and Paul Volcker

Glossary

Board of Governors of the Federal Reserve System: The group of individuals who are in charge of the 12 Federal Reserve Banks that comprise the Federal Reserve System.

Chair of the Federal Reserve Board of Governors: The top person at the United States central bank (the bank that is in charge of monitoring a country's money supply), who makes sure that people have jobs, access to money, and monitors the cost of goods.

Council of Economic Advisors: A United States agency within the Executive Office of the President established in 1946, which advises the President of the United States on economic policy.

Economics: A study of how people make decisions to use money and resources.

Federal Reserve System: The central bank of the United States that monitors the economy and serves the public interest.

Job: The work someone does in exchange for money.

Paycheck: Money given in exchange for work.

Professors: Teachers in college.

Time Line

1946
Janet is born in Brooklyn, New York

1949
Janet, 3, poses with her big brother, John

1967
Janet graduates summa cum laude from Brown University with a degree in Economics

1971-1976
Janet works as an assistant professor of economics at Harvard University

1977
Janet works as a staff economist at the Board of Governors of the Federal Reserve System

1978
Janet and George marry

1963
Janet graduates as valedictorian from Fort Hamilton High School in Brooklyn, NY and attends Brown University in Providence, Rhode Island

1971
Janet, the only woman in her class, receives her doctorate in Economics from Yale University

1974
In the summer, Janet is a visiting economist at the Federal Reserve Board of Governors in Washington D.C.

1977
Janet meets her husband, George Akerlof, an economist, in the cafeteria at the Federal Reserve Board of Governors

1979
Janet and George move to London to teach at the London School of Economics and Political Science

Janet teaches economics to undergraduate and graduate students at the University of California Berkeley's Haas School of Business

1982
Janet receives tenure as a professor at University of California Berkeley

1997

President Bill Clinton nominates Janet to serve as Chair of the Council of Economic Advisors in the White House, where she serves until 1999

2004
Janet is appointed President and CEO of the Federal Reserve Bank of San Francisco

2014
Janet becomes the first woman to chair the Board of Governors of the Federal Reserve System

2021

Janet is the first woman to be nominated and confirmed as United States Treasury Secretary

1981
Janet and George welcome son, Robby

1999-2004
Janet returns to the University of California Berkley's Haas School of Business with a joint appointment in the Department of Economics

Janet joins the Brookings Institution as a Distinguished Fellow in Residence

2018

1994
President Bill Clinton nominates Janet to the Federal Reserve Board of Governors

2010
Janet is sworn in as the Vice Chair of the Board of Governors

CPSIA information can be obtained
at www.ICGtesting.com
Printed in the USA
BVHW011522020523
663427BV00004B/120